D1555571

Published by: Health Communications, Inc.
1721 Blount Road, Suite #1
Pompano Beach, Florida 33069

Copyright ©1985, Marie Schutt. All Rights Reserved.

No part of this publication may be reproduced, stored in a retrieval system, or transmitted in any form, or by any means, electronic, mechanical, photocopying, recording, or otherwise, without the written permission of the publisher.

Published in the United States of America.

ISBN 0-932194-31-1

DEDICATION

For my son, Garry, the most courageous man I have ever known.

ACKNOWLEDGMENTS

Wives of Alcoholics was a joint venture with many people helping me. To them, I would like to say "Thank you."

To my husband, Harold, Director of Providence, for giving me the setting and freedom for the background material.

To Sandy Erickson, for her faith in the book, and her skill in editing.

To Marcy Walker, for her hours of working on the manuscript.

To the entire staff at Providence for their support and help.

To Mark Worden, for his patience and skill in editing.

To all the co-dependent women who have contributed to this work, the recovering ones and those who still suffer, in the hope of better tomorrows.

Marie Schutt
1985

TABLE OF CONTENTS

INTRODUCTION

This book is about any woman who marries an alcoholic: The co-dependent wife. As she tries desperately to communicate her own needs and aspirations, she is constantly put down and rejected. She grieves broken dreams and broken promises. She creates unrealistic hopes and expectations.

The co-dependent wife lives in a world of excited misery, careening from crisis to crisis in reaction to her husband's alcoholic behavior. No pattern for prosperity develops in her home. The money that might have gone into savings for a house, the money that might have been set aside for a special vacation or for some other dream—the money slips away as her husband continues to drink, and as his drinking affects his job, his health and the well-being of the whole family.

Her own unmet needs, and those of her children, add to the stress created by her husband's alcoholic behavior.

As she lives with a chemically-addicted person, the co-dependent develops her own addictions—to sensation, security, and power. Day after day, she becomes more rigid and indecisive. She forgets how to laugh and play. Love for her husband becomes a millstone around her neck. She learns the meaning of despair and leads a life of desperation, turbulent and anxiety-ridden.

However, the co-dependent wife can change her addictions to preferences. She can make choices for her own well-being. She can expect her loved one to become responsible for his own recovery. She can become a fulfilled woman, a responsible, flexible choicemaker.

This book is about the co-dependent wife, as she learns to love, and as she learns to detach and truly live.

This book is about...

● Sandra, a lady of great courage. (The examples that follow are real; the names of the individuals are not.) Sandra works as an investment consultant and has three young children at home. She attends all their school functions and ball games. She is a gourmet cook. Her appearance is always faultless, and her home orderly. And she is also tense, anxious and critical of her family. She is constantly over-extended and over-achieving. Sandra is married to an alcoholic.

● Kelly, intelligent and hardworking. But she has difficulty holding a job. She can't get along with her employers and fellow workers. At home, she is often abusive with her children, but insists, at the same time, that they have all the material advantages. Kelly is angry, frustrated and irritated most of the time. Kelly is married to an alcoholic.

● Dorothy, a quiet, unassuming woman. She is often seen as "a saint" or "such a good person." She is long-suffering and seemingly compliant. Dorothy actually rules her family with guilt and martyrdom. Her children strongly defend her actions and protect her from their father. Dorothy feels threatened and fearful most of the time. She worries about everything—money, illness, and how others see her. At the same time, Dorothy is very careful to try to preserve the appearance of normalcy. Dorothy is married to an alcoholic.

● Debbie lives on welfare. Some of her children have been taken away from her because of neglect. She has never worked consistently and has no job skills. She has a ninth-grade education. She is shy and anxious. She feels discouraged and hopeless. Debbie was married to an alcoholic.

● Tammy and her small child live with her brother and his family. Her brother supports them both. Tammy has given up seeking work and spends most of her time watching TV. She spends her evenings in a bar with her drinking friends. Her brother is angry at her for not taking more responsibility, but he is unwilling to see Tammy's child suffer. Tammy has little self-esteem and cannot make decisions. Tammy was involved with an alcoholic.

These are the co-dependents, the women whose lives have been drastically affected by the alcoholism of a partner, a spouse, a lover.

Let's take a look at co-dependency, the problem, and the process.

1
The Problem: Co-Dependency

Wives of alcoholics are often the first to seek professional help for their husbands' drinking problems. Wives of alcoholics are especially sensitive to alcohol problems, because over 50% of the women who marry alcoholics were raised in alcoholic homes—homes in which one or more family members are chemically dependent.

Exposed to alcoholic behavior at an early age, this wife of an alcoholic does not learn co-dependency in her new home —she comes into her marriage with a whole repertoire of survival skills and co-dependent strategies.

She learned, early on, how to cope with the alcoholism of a parent, and she carries the learnings into her adult relationships. In effect, the bride of an alcoholic sets up new family systems that allow her to continue the co-dependency that she learned from her own childhood and youth.

As the husband adapts to alcohol, the wife develops a kind of addiction to his behavior, a **Co-Dependency.** What exactly is this co-dependency? It's **the process of one person standing between an alcoholic and the crisis caused by drinking. It's a protective stance adopted by the spouse that keeps the husband from experiencing the consequences of his drinking.**

The Conspiracy of Silence

Chemical dependency flourishes in an atmosphere of tacit acceptance created by what seems to be a "conspiracy" of silence on the part of the addict's family, employer and friends. Here's how this tacit acceptance of alcoholism works:

1. *The Co-Dependent Wife's Silence*

As the alcoholic gradually moves deeper into his illness, the co-dependent wife begins to find the relationship less and less rewarding. With recurring disappointments, her anger and resentment increase. But she doesn't let anyone know. She may display these feelings at home, but she keeps them carefully hidden from the rest of the world—hidden from anyone who might think badly of her. The co-dependent wife may complain to family and friends, but she learns to keep quiet when around those who might suggest that she find ways to change the situation. At this point, she is seeking sympathy, not empathy. She does not see the usage as the problem, but instead sees the rejection and discounting by the one she loves as the problem. She takes it personally. To her, it's a reflection on the worth of the relationship.

2. *The Co-Dependent and the Employer*

The co-dependent has two reasons for protecting her husband in his place of employment. She wants the boss to approve of her mate, and she fears the insecurity of unemployment. In her childhood, she was often frightened by her alcoholic parent's inability to hold a job. She plays this old tape in her own marriage.

The co-dependent wife is usually faced with one of two situations in regard to her husband's employer: (a) the boss either drinks with the alcoholic husband, or likes the alcoholic and sees nothing wrong with the usage: and, (b) the employer gets angry and upset by the increasing usage, and even threatens to terminate the employment. In either case, she is forced into a conspiracy of silence.

3. *The Co-Dependent and Friends*
Unhappy and feeling rejected, the co-dependent finds solace with friends who also feel unhappy and neglected. Get-togethers become complaint sessions—almost a kind of "recreational grumbling." The co-dependent learns to avoid talking about her feelings with friends or relatives who suggest ways of solving problems. She wants friends who will not threaten the status quo. She's more interested in vindication than in resolving the family problems.

As she concentrates all of her energies on controlling His Drinking, she has less and less ability to see that her own behavior is contributing to the problem. She feels discounted and rejected, and believes that he is deliberately treating her badly. The co-dependent remains totally unaware of what **she** is doing.

New Dimensions of Chemical Dependency
Chemical dependence—dependence on any drug, including alcohol—is widely recognized as a disease. It strikes one in ten people who drink. It is no respector of age, sex, creed or race. Chemical dependency has pre-existing conditions, a predictable course, and if uncontrolled, is terminal.

In the last few years, a new dimension of the illness emerged. There's increasing evidence that genetic factors are involved and that chemical dependency is a trans-generational disorder.

Two features of chemical dependency stand out: the use of a chemical to change feelings and perceptions of reality (the chemical high); and, the behavior that results from a need to keep the body in a drug-altered condition. This need has an impact on family, friends, work and community involvement.

It is impossible for others to live in this stressful environment without reacting to it. Each member of the family learns survival behavior in a home filled with destructive role-modeling and inconsistency. They learn to control the little area immediately around them with methods that are not necessarily personally rewarding.

The pattern that emerges is predictable, progressive, and massively damaging to relationships—all relationships.

2
The Co-Dependent

Alcoholism is first seen in deterioration of personal relationships, then in financial problems, and often in legal involvement, including DWI and divorce. Its victims display symptoms of the illness in denying that anything is wrong, emotional isolation from others, high stress in the home, and impaired judgment regarding family, finances and job.

The woman who lives with the alcoholic develops an enabling illness. She constantly stands between the alcoholic and his crises, thus enabling and condoning the further usage of the drug. Her illness is predictable in its inception, and its course runs narrow lines to a specific ending. It develops high stress in its victim, causing other physical illnesses in its progress. This women is denied her birthright of marital companionship and rewarding development as a wife and mother.

She does not intentionally set out to marry an alcoholic. She

5

did not plan her life to be full of anxiety, fear and stress. She did not plan to deprive her children of effective role-modeling. The co-dependent is as much a victim of alcoholism as her mate.

The alcoholic's addiction becomes a third entity in their relationship. She even gives it a name: **His Drinking.**
His Drinking becomes her primary topic of conversation and it affects everything she does.

His Drinking is a dreaded and unwelcome guest at holidays and special family events. The fear of His Drinking ruins special occasions and casts a pall of apprehension over all other days.

His Drinking and Sexual Fulfillment

Nowhere does His Drinking intrude more disastrously than in the bedroom. As the alcoholic becomes more physically and financially involved with his addiction, the cost to the marital relationship becomes very high. It is difficult for a woman to put aside the anger, frustration and emotional turmoil of the waking hours and become transformed at night into an amorous bedfellow.

Some co-dependent wives react with revulsion at the prospect of sex when His Drinking rears its ugly head. As one wife said, "It's hard to be romantic when your partner's drunk and reeks with booze and cigarettes."

Other wives engage in the sexual act with a disinterested resignation and anorgasmic acquiescence: "It's easier, less hassle, to just go ahead and get it over as quickly as possible." Of course, that's only part of the problem. Shakespeare eloquently pointed out years ago, "Liquor provokes desire, but takes away the performance." Performance declines as His Drinking continues, and sex becomes a dreaded, pleasureless chore.

Finally, many co-dependent wives react to His Drinking with rejection and sexual indifference. "Why bother?" His Drinking drives an insurmountable wedge into the man-woman relationship. As long as His Drinking shares the bedroom with them, a rewarding physical and emotional relationship cannot exist.

Guilt and Beyond

The alcoholic has a tremendous ability to transfer the guilt he feels onto those who love him. His wife is usually the most eager recipient, because she already feels emotions that conflict with her values of a rewarding family system. She has been angry, sulking, silent, and screaming—all to no avail.

The co-dependent wife is eager to believe she is in control. She will attempt to have everything perfect in the home. She tries desperately to be a perfect wife and a perfect mother, and she conveys a sense of tense perfectionism to her children. Her unspoken thoughts: "If only I make our life as perfect as possible, His Drinking will vanish."

But since her behavior is not the real cause of His Drinking, all of her attempts to make him quit drinking end in dismal failure. The consequence? Frustration. And guilt. Whatever she does, it isn't enough, it doesn't have any impact on His Drinking.

The co-dependent wife finds herself in a no-win situation, "damned if she does and damned if she doesn't." Many wives of alcoholics refer to this behavior as "walking on eggs when he is around."

The wife who accepts this transference of guilt sets up an unrealistic hope that things will get better, that His Drinking will magically abate, and a happy home life will ensue. This hope, which becomes her enemy, may endure for years, fed on illusions and small promises of change.

Only when the co-dependent wife realizes that she never had any control over His Drinking, does a recovery process begin. She can finally see that a change in her attitudes and behavior may result in his accepting responsibility for the control of his own illness. She must also see that he needs to learn to be totally abstinent. One drink is a relapse for him.

It is frightening and difficult for the co-dependent wife to change. Her self-worth is low and her faith in her ability to

7

make decisions has been shattered.

She feels that she has violated her own value system by fighting, lying, covering up and neglecting the children. She feels inadequate as a wife, as a mother, and as a woman. But once she understands that she is not responsible for His Drinking, she can start to see herself in a new light. And she can begin the slow healing process of recovery. She understands that **she was not responsible for his illness,** but has a responsibility to stop protecting or condoning it.

She begins to detach herself from His Drinking. She detaches herself from the alcoholic's behavior. She stops harshly judging herself and starts rewarding herself for small victories. Her children begin to react differently as her own behavior changes, and recovery starts in the family.

At the same time, the co-dependent wife cannot be sure of what the alcoholic will do under these new circumstances.

Many, many alcoholics do nothing. They continue drinking and they die.

Once the co-dependent wife has made a decision about her own life, the alcoholic is faced with a decision about His Drinking. Since alcoholism cannot exist, except in an atmosphere of tacit acceptance that perpetuates His Drinking, the alcoholic must decide to become abstinent as the family changes, or he must find a new situation, apart from his family—a situation that condones and encourages His Drinking.

It is not an easy decision for the co-dependent wife. She's filled with anxiety and insecurity. ("How will I support my kids? I can't just let him kill himself. What about the bills? What about his parents and my own?")

The woman who lives with him, and loves him, cannot know what he will choose to do. And that's the dilemma. She can only decide to change her own unrewarding lifestyle for one that is nurturing and fruitful for herself and her children. But she must change without knowing what his decision will be.

These faltering steps toward independence, health and sanity may be the most difficult thing she ever does in her life.

Women living with alcoholics develop specific patterns and roles in the disease process. If they were raised in an alcoholic or high-stress home, they learned certain survival behaviors in childhood, and these coping responses carry over into adulthood.

Some women come from functional families that were relatively happy and stress-free. Yet, if they too, fall in love with an alcoholic, they are at risk for developing the dysfunctional behavior that characterizes co-dependent wives.

In the sections that follow, we'll look at a variety of survival roles. Keep in mind that these roles are not hardened, rigid categories. They are useful ways to describe behavior, and it is important to see that roles are potentially open and fluid, with movement across roles as situations change, and as the disease progresses or recovery begins.

Jael Greenleaf, Timmen Cermak, and Sharon Wegscheider-Cruse have explored the behavior of family members who are raised in chemically dependent, or high-stress, homes. From their observations have come a set of symptoms or patterns which can be used as guidelines to understand the predictable behavior of grown-up co-dependents as they move into adult relationships.

In her writings and workshops, Sharon Wegscheider-Cruse talks about the childhood roles of Hero, Scapegoat, Lost Child, and Family Mascot. In this book, the adult counterparts of these childhood roles become: Caretaker, Rebel, Passive, and Youthful Co-Dependents. These adult roles will be discussed in more detail in later chapters.

But first, let's examine the role of the spouse from a functional birth home, the woman who just happens to marry an alcoholic. How does she adjust to the baffling abnormal lifestyle that comes as a result of His Drinking?

3

The Wife From the Nurturing Family

The wife of the alcoholic is often the first person to seek help. She does not seek help for herself, but wants to find a way to interrupt His Drinking. She is certain that drinking is the cause of the problem, and if she can find a "cure"—find a way to get her husband to go on the wagon—then everything else will be all right.

When she is finally at the point of divorce, she reaches out in one last frantic effort to change her husband's lifestyle. At this juncture, she is unable to judge her own actions. If she is challenged to look at her behavior, she reacts defensively, because she has lost (or maybe she never had) the ability to detach from the behavior of the alcoholic. She feels that she is right and he is wrong.

Some of the wives of alcoholics have lost the ability to detach. Others have never developed it. The co-dependent wife who has lost the ability to detach comes originally from a functional, nurturing home. The wife who never developed the ability to detach generally comes from an alcoholic family or a high-stress home.

While each co-dependent wife adapts to the behavior of the alcoholic over a period of time, the recovery process varies according to the wife's childhood background. The behavior learned in childhood, in the family of origin, carries over into adulthood. Thus, the co-dependent wife who grew up in an alcoholic family, or in a high-stress home environment, has no framework for normal family interaction.

On the other hand, the wife from a functional, nurturing background will struggle, but will eventually re-establish functional behavior. She has forgotten, but not lost, normalcy in family relationships. Although she will develop dysfunctional enabling characteristics while living with the alcoholic, she can re-establish nurturing value systems and communications.

The difference between the two co-dependency styles is apparent in the recovery process. When the spouse from a functional background is given permission to feel that her inclinations and perceptions are valid, she will move more rapidly toward a healthy recovery. Dorothy exemplifies this type of recovery.

Dorothy was brought up in a loving, nurturing home. While attending college in San Francisco, she met and married Bob, who came from a chemically dependent home. Bob's drinking soon manifested the symptoms of alcoholism—personal and family irresponsibility, emotional isolation and denial.

For several years, Dorothy tried to establish communications and nurturing values in the family. After 23 years of emotional turmoil, she sought help. Dorothy was at the end of her rope. "I was frustrated, angry and on the verge of tears most of the time," she recalls. "And although I knew it wasn't my fault, I felt responsible for my husband's drinking."

Dorothy didn't suffer in martyred silence. She screamed and fought and sulked over the years. But, the main impact was that she violated her own sense of values and diminished her self-worth.

Positive changes began to occur as soon as Dorothy learned about the disease of chemical dependency. She also learned what it meant to be co-dependent—but, most importantly, she learned to detach from her husband's alcoholic behavior.

Dorothy discovered another important fact: If she changed her behavior, it would have an impact on her husband's behavior. However, the change entailed a risk. There would be no way to predict accurately how her husband would respond. He might accept help. But, then again, he might also remain defiant and terminate the relationship.

Dorothy accepted the risk and learned to detach from the situation. Her own recovery was remarkably swift. In three months, she looked ten years younger, and she discovered how to laugh again. Her children began to respond more positively to her, but her husband decided to leave. She let him go, knowing that she would still be willing to help him at any time in the future. She also knew that if he were not willing to seek help for his drinking problem, she could no longer live with him. Alcoholism cannot exist in a functional home, where the partner refuses to be permissive and passive toward His Drinking.

The wife who grows up in a non-alcoholic home environment adapts to chemical dependency in the same way as a wife who was raised in a home where there is chemical dependency in one or more of the family members. She will ...

1. Develop, with family and friends, a conspiracy of silence around the husband's chemical dependency.
2. Accept unrealistic responsibility in financial matters.
3. Pay more attention to the alcoholic than to the welfare of her children.

4. Develop stress-related illnesses, such as hypertension, ulcers, chronic anxiety, headaches, digestive disease, blood sugar anomalies, angina, and ironically, addiction to pills or alcohol.
5. Become isolated from friends and relatives as a result of feelings of shame and low self-worth.
6. Live in a crisis-oriented world, where frantic, hectic behavior is the norm.
7. Make constant decisions that are detrimental to her and her children.
8. Lose her sense of humor.
9. Indulge in fantasies about the good life.
10. Lose her ability to enjoy natural highs.

The co-dependent wife from a relatively normal family learned in childhood to enjoy natural highs resulting from family, school, job and friends. She developed self-esteem. And, she enters new relationships believing that these qualities will be forthcoming rewards.

Indeed, she finds that the early years of marriage are often rewarding. His Drinking has not yet overshadowed the natural highs, the rewards of family life, and the co-dependent wife understandably believes that the good times will continue.

Later, she will tearfully remember this era of good feelings. She will try desperately to return to them. She fails again and again to reinstate the good times past. But hope springs eternal, and unrealistic hope is one of the main characteristics of the co-dependent wife.

Ellen also grew up in a non-alcoholic home. She was raised on a ranch. Her mother and father both worked hard, but they found ways to spend quality time with Ellen and her brothers and sisters. Consequently, the children developed strong values: Honesty; responsibility; and hard work. They also knew how to enjoy playing, and how to share with each other.

When Ellen met Tom and married him, she saw only his charm. She was oblivious to the irresponsibility that lay behind his charming exterior. As his drinking worsened during the course of their marriage, Ellen became an over-achiever, trying to keep the family going and, at the same time, trying to retain fragments of her own self-worth.

Ellen found herself reacting to Tom's drinking in ways that violated her own values of honesty and family closeness.

She gave birth to three children, and she began to feel trapped in the situation. Ellen tried to keep her family from finding out how bad things were—Tom's drinking was bad enough, but she was especially embarrassed about the financial crisis that was the result of it.

Tom's own insecurity forced her away from her family's functions. Over and over, they planned reunions and holidays that they never attended. Tom's behavior would precipitate a financial crisis which kept them from going. Ellen began to believe that he disliked her family, when in reality he felt uneasy and unsure of himself around them.

Tom had also entered the stage of his illness when protecting his ability to drink was more important than the family welfare. He could not control the amount he could drink when he visited Ellen's family, so he made sure that he and Ellen did not go there.

A television program on alcoholism gave Ellen the incentive to seek help. She saw ways to change, and she began to detach from Tom's chemical dependency. Predictably, her changes disturbed and threatened Tom. He went to treatment to find out what was going on. He stayed to recover.

The whole family learned to communicate and express their own needs and feelings. They learned how to laugh and to love. They learned how to share with each other. They all moved into the recovery process.

The Dynamics of Co-Dependency

In every instance of co-dependency, we see common features: As the disease of chemical dependency progresses, and the alcoholic becomes increasingly isolated, the spouse tries harder to get the relationship back to normal. She cannot see that it never was normal, and she evolves a pervasive system of denial that resembles the denial used by the alcoholic.

The co-dependent wife denies that anything is wrong in the family. And, at the same time, she frantically searches for the magic fix that will reinstate the good times of the past.

She begins to feel increasingly rejected and unloved. Feeling depressed and abandoned, she becomes negative and bitter. She nags her husband and children. Her negativity gives the alcoholic an excuse to withdraw further into chemical dependency and emotional isolation.

The vicious cycle of recrimination and withdrawal undermines the family, and leads ultimately to the collapse of the marital relationship.

Her anger and hurt make affection and sexual intimacy almost impossible. The alcoholic begins to have difficulty with sexual performance, and blames it onto his wife's hostility and negative attitudes. His drinking often makes him repugnant to her. He withdraws and finds more accepting friends outside the home. She feels angry, rejected and bitter.

Anger and bitterness conflict with the co-dependent wife's value system, and she begins to feel that she really is the blameworthy partner. The conditions for guilt transference are in place and working smoothly.

Even so, the co-dependent wife believes that it is in her power to control His Drinking. The alcoholic has convinced her that his behavior is a direct consequence of her actions. She clings to this belief, because she wants her life to be different, and if she is to blame, then, obviously, she can make things better by being a perfect wife, or a perfect mother. When her attempt at perfection does not stop the progression of her husband's chemical dependency, she becomes frustrated and frightened. She then redoubles her efforts, and increases the stress in the home.

Her illusion of control persists through many crises, and

only when she seeks help does she realize that she was **never** in control of the situation.

It is important to remember one fact: **Alcoholism can only exist in the home that develops these conditions.** In the crisis-oriented home, the co-dependent wife becomes less and less confident in her ability to judge nurturing behavior. She swings from one extreme to the other, in an attempt to establish normalcy as she understands it.

The alcoholic uses her indecision to prove that her actions are causing his drinking. At the same time, he distances himself from his wife and children. He really believes that his wife, his children and his job cause him to drink. In order for recovery to take place, the alcoholic must realize that external conditions do not cause His Drinking. He must realize that usage of the drug, rather than external circumstances, is at the root of his alcoholism, and the family problems stemming from his chemical dependency.

Again: **Alcoholism in the home must include dysfunctional reactions from the co-dependent wife for the illness to progress.**

Hard Choices: To Stay or Not To Stay

If the wife is able to maintain the values of self-worth she had at the beginning of her marriage, alcoholism cannot take root and flourish. The relationship will usually end in five to seven years. It ends when the good times are definitely gone.

The wife may try to change His Drinking, try to alter the emerging pattern of alcoholism. But, when she finally finds her efforts are futile, she will withdraw. And more and more frequently, she will leave.

On the other hand, if the home situation does not continue to be a place where he can drink—a sanctuary that protects His Drinking—then he may be the one to leave.

The wife who maintains self-worth usually seeks a non-alcoholic in her next relationship. She knows the harm that can come from marriage to an alcoholic, and she does not want to repeat the agony. She wants to protect herself and her children. (Even so, her children may develop addictions as they mature, since there are genetic factors at work, and they have been exposed in childhood to the stresses and insecurities of chemical dependency.)

What happens to the co-dependent wife who remains in a deteriorating relationship with an alcoholic husband? For one thing, she accepts an unrealistic financial responsibility.

She controls the finances in an effort to control His Drinking. If there is little money available for the purchase of alcohol, she thinks, then he will not be able to continue his alcoholic behavior. She will budget money for His Drinking, and when financial crises occur, she makes up the difference by bringing in extra income. "It's only temporary," she says, overlooking the fact that the pattern occurs again and again.

"I will never buy alcohol for him," she firmly vows. But she works to pay the rent while he spends their money for His Drinking.

The co-dependent wife seldom has an accurate idea of the amount of money he spends on His Drinking. As she adapts to financial crises from month-to-month, she may even begin to realize that she has no idea what her husband's wages are. She doesn't find this too unusual. They are not communicating much on any level.

Still, she worries. She studies the tax forms, and she looks through his wallet for extra money or pay stubs.

The conspiracy of silence in the alcoholic family does not allow her to be direct. She can't admit there is a problem, so how on earth can she demand her husband to be open about financial matters?

A prosperity pattern for investment and pleasure-spending does not develop in the alcoholic home. The money spent for drinking precludes prosperity and causes crisis financing. The co-dependent wife copes with threatening calls from creditors. She sees her children suffer from material and emotional

17

deprivation. And she herself reaps no financial reward, and experiences meager gratification in the marriage. Yet her upbringing has stressed the importance of financial responsibility, so for self-protection, she moves into denial and isolation ... and she continues to violate her most cherished values.

Often religion or church activities become havens for the co-dependent wife. When she takes the children to church once a week, she is able to maintain the pretense for a short time that the family is all right, even though the alcoholic is not present. The outward appearance of normalcy becomes extremely important.

But this has a mixed impact on the children. Many times they come to judge the co-dependent wife and mother harshly. "She's nothing but a hypocrite," they charge. They see clearly that her actions and her verbal messages are inconsistent, and the children end up confused and full of resentment.

Sometimes the co-dependent wife develops a partnership with one of the children to make up for growing isolation and lack of communication with her alcoholic husband. She takes the child into her confidence, often sharing complex problems that are beyond the child's capacity to understand. The child reacts with an exaggerated sense of maturity, trying to be all the things that are lacking in the alcoholic.

The child becomes, in effect, a little adult. The co-dependent mother accepts him as an adult, and he strives to behave like one.

The result? The child loses precious years of childhood. He becomes responsible for brothers and sisters. He worries about finances. He is rewarded by his mother's approval and continuing need for his support and companionship. Yet, she repeatedly rejects him when she returns to her compulsive involvement with the alcoholic.

Children in alcoholic homes almost always blame the non-drinker for the persisting conditions. They feel that the co-dependent wife has the ability to change the situation, and yet she does nothing. The children hide their growing frustration and resentment, until it periodically erupts with shouting and blaming. Feeling trapped and abused, the children begin making plans to leave home as soon as possible ... one way or another.

The children fleeing this kind of home carry with them the key ingredients for alcoholism and co-dependency, and high-stress home environments in their own adult relationships and homes.

The wife who grew up in a nurturing home comes into an alcoholic relationship with high hopes. She plans for a prosperous and rewarding life. She sticks with it—stays in an untenable relationship—until self-preservation and concern for the welfare of her children force her out.

Some wives are so trapped by their own co-dependency that they endure His Drinking for years, staying after the children have grown and left home—almost as if the burdens of living with an alcoholic are more rewarding than the risks of making a new life.

The wife who remains while the disease progresses and the relationship deteriorates sometimes gets a legal divorce. She may then continue for years in an emotional entanglement with her alcoholic husband and His Drinking. She will force him to leave home. Then she takes him back when he penitently returns promising, "I won't do it again. Honest, honey. Never again."

What makes her think it will be different? Hope springs eternal, and she clings to the irrational hope that maybe, just maybe, something will change. Grasping at straws, she says, "Well, at least I didn't marry him again." She sees this as an improvement.

She may refuse to live with him, but stays constantly involved with the crises in his life. She usually stays involved sexually, although much of the caring has vanished, and there is little expectation that he will remain faithful. The extent of the co-dependent wife's illness may be judged from the fact that she does not think there is anything unusual about this relationship.

Since alcoholism shortens the life-span of its victims, the co-dependent wife usually outlives the alcoholic. At last, freed from the turmoil of an alcoholic relationship, she continues to be dysfunctional with her children. And frequently she seeks out another alcoholic partner.

Moving Towards Recovery

Increasingly, spouses seek help for themselves. The co-dependent wife who has the courage to seek help has every chance for recovery for herself and her children. The change in her is the best chance that the alcoholic has for personal recovery.

When she takes the initiative, she breaks the conspiracy of silence. She admits, "Everything is **not** all right. Our family is **not** functioning well. His Drinking is **not** social drinking. I am **not** happy with the way things are."

And she admits that she is powerless over His Drinking, the most important step of all.

First, the co-dependent wife learns that she needs help in understanding both alcoholism and her own co-dependency. She must take a hard look at her own addictive behavior. She must accept that she is not responsible for its inception, but that she does have a responsibility to end it.

She must understand that she cannot continue to play games in the relationship—that she must take decisive action. And she must realize that action on her part may result in the alcoholic's seeking help. Or, it may result in the end of the relationship. This may be the most painful and difficult choice she will ever face.

She must also understand that if he does not confront his illness, he will likely die of it, and she cannot change this fact. She must resolve to save her own life, and the lives of her children, no matter what decision the alcoholic makes. She must see that his decision not to make a decision is actually a choice (albeit a sick one), that allows his illness to continue. She can set up conditions that force him to consider alternatives, but she has no ability to control the outcome. Only the alcoholic can make the decision to recover. And, as everyone knows, far too many alcoholics simply do not make this choice.

The wife who decides to change her lifestyle can usually benefit from a support system of professional chemical dependency counseling, and involvement with Al-Anon to help her through the rough times of detaching, of loving and letting go. She will experience fear and loneliness and confusion. She will be convinced that she has made a horrible mistake. "Maybe it really wasn't as bad as I thought it was," she tells herself. "Maybe I exaggerated His Drinking problems. Maybe I should have just let things alone."

She has serious doubts about her decision to detach and to fulfill her own needs. There are natural feelings in the early stages of recovery, and the wife needs guidance and support as she sorts out her real feelings from the old patterns of feeling what she's supposed to feel.

The alcoholic will react to her changes in behavior in one of two ways: He will try to convince her that he really can quit or control His Drinking. The promise of a return to the good times has worked in the past. And, since she's primed to hope, she is apt to accept this ploy of reinstating the old rules. Once the status quo is re-established, the alcoholic returns to drinking.

However, he may also react with anger and threats of aggression. In the past, he may have been very successful in controlling the behavior of other family members with his anger. The wife may be truly afraid of her husband. She may see him as being capable of physical violence. She is not merely psychologically intimidated, for in many homes battered wives can attest to the reality of the threat of violence. This kind of control is especially useful in restoring the familiar routines the alcoholic has come to depend on.

During these trying times, the wife must remain firm in her commitment to change. If she sees physical danger, she must have a safe place for herself and her children. It may be necessary to take legal precautions for her own safety. His bullying behavior—whether bluster or not—must not be passively condoned.

The wife begins her recovery when she decides to change her attitudes about His Drinking and her marriage. She must accept the fact that she is in an intolerable situation, and that she has the ability to change it. She must accept the bleak reality that things may worsen temporarily, as the alcoholic tries to maintain the environment that allows him to continue drinking.

She must accept the fact that the children will be confused by changes in routines and rules, and mainly by violating the conspiracy of silence. The kids may become disruptive and unruly, and the wife must be prepared to deal with them, as well as with her husband.

But she will find that a change in her behavior is the catalyst that starts new happenings in the family. The children will watch with wonder, but no trust. They have been disappointed too many times.

As the new situation unfolds, and the wife stays firm in her decision to detach from the alcoholic's behavior, the children will begin to communicate with her. The alcoholic will become more confused as the old boundaries dissolve. He will decide to seek help or to leave. A growing number of alcoholics seek help.

The wife and family of the alcoholic can recover, especially if they are persistent in the search for health and sanity. With the help of family support systems, Al-Anon and counseling, families can, and do, recover.

4

The Caretaker Co-Dependent

The Caretaker Co-Dependent is usually one of the older children in the family, if not the oldest. She often leaves the alcoholic home, only to marry an alcoholic. Growing up in a crisis-oriented environment, where relationships were strained and communication distorted, she learned how to survive. She learned the rules that later motivated her to seek out a similar situation.

THE COVERT RULES

- Peace at any price
- Maintain the conspiracy of silence
- Never quit
- Go to any lengths to be "right"
- Never discuss feelings
- Try to seem normal

The Caretaker Co-Dependent will use a combination of these rules, as long as she lives in the new alcoholic situation. Since she has no basis for functional family behavior, and no working experience with family consistency, she looks at other homes for guidelines.

Her perception of functional families, however, is colored by her childhood experiences. She idealizes other families that appear to be trouble-free. Her efforts to control her own family always fall short of ideal, so she constantly searches for new models, new solutions. In doing so, the Caretaker Co-Dependent displays indecision and creates inconsistency. This adds to the uncertainty and unpredictability in the new alcoholic home.

The Caretaker Co-Dependent fails time after time to make things better by her rigid, over-achieving efforts. And her failures compound her sense of low self-worth.

Protecting His Drinking

Anna is a Caretaker Co-Dependent. She came from an abusive home. Her alcoholic father either beat her or ignored her. She decided, as a child, that her own children would not be treated this way.

When her son, John, developed chemical dependency, Anna refused to see his problem. She made excuses for his behavior and accepted his irresponsible behavior. At 29 years of age, John still lives at home. "I need to get my old bills paid off," he says. But he keeps on drinking and using drugs. And he does not contribute to the household finances.

During one drinking episode, John drove his car into the garbage cans in the driveway. Anna responded by replacing the garbage cans. She put them in new racks on the opposite side of the house, away from the driveway. The garbage cans would be safe from John, and John would not have to worry about hitting the garbage cans again when he came home drunk. She saw nothing unusual in her actions.

Anna has bailed her son out of jail, paid his bills, supported his children, and put up with his constant verbal abuse. To outsiders, her behavior seems bizarre. "Why on earth does she put up with that sort of thing?" they wonder.

But her reactions toward John must be viewed in the context of her childhood experiences, and the decisions she made as a result of growing up in an alcoholic home. Anna is determined not to treat John as she was treated by her father.

The conspiracy of silence carried over from her home of origin keeps her unaware that John's behavior is quite different from her own when she was a child. She was responsible, but she does not expect responsibility from her son. She keeps expecting him to realize his faults, and to make the necessary changes without any pressure. She really believes that at some magic age, he will suddenly develop responsibility.

Anna could have maintained this role for years. But John was finally sent to treatment through a court order. Anna went with him to a family program. She had great difficulty accepting the fact that her own behavior was enabling John to continue his illness. After all, wasn't she doing everything in her power to help him?

Gradually, Anna began to see that her "help" really wasn't help at all. She saw that in her Caretaker role, she was overly protective of John. She saw that John had adapted to her caretaking by allowing her to take care of him, and by learning that she would always take responsibility for helping him out of a jam. Anna became John's ace-in-the-hole.

Like other Caretakers, Anna gets her sense of self-worth from the things she does for others. She is long-suffering and maintains the helper role beyond all normal boundaries. But even Anna felt that she was being pushed to the limit by her son's drinking. From time to time, she made threats: "If he drinks once more, he will have to leave."

But when John drank again, she always found an excuse, a plausible reason to condone it. "Next time," she said. "One more time, and that's it. I just can't put up with it anymore.

He'll have to leave." It was always next time. Next time.

Anna was also a controller. She could see that her attempts to control were not working, but she couldn't quit. Quitting meant failure, defeat. So Anna stubbornly kept trying to control a situation that was not within her ability to control.

She felt that she couldn't make mistakes, and she went to great lengths to be "right." Since her feelings of self-worth came from external sources, she had difficulty accepting criticism, and she had difficulty being self-critical. A mistake represented a flaw in her basic character, rather than a normal human failing.

This need to control, to always be in command, causes great stress in the alcoholic home, adding to the tension and turmoil caused by the alcoholic.

The Caretaker makes plans to do far more than could be done in any normal day. She has little ability to say "No!" to anyone outside of her home. She desperately needs the approval of others, and they, in turn, bolster her self-worth by seeing her as a good, giving person.

Unfortunately, in her own home, the Caretaker often discounts her own small children's needs, and they feel as if they are not as important to her as other people are. Eager to be admired and respected, she freely volunteers her husband's and children's services without consulting them, giving no consideration to their wants or desires. The Caretaker honestly does not see what she is doing to her family.

The Caretaker behaves ambivalently toward the alcoholic in the family. At home, she shows disapproval by word and action—or by giving him the "silent treatment," a stance usually reserved for non-persons. She allows her children to see her contempt toward the alcoholic, seeking their approval and alliance against him.

At the same time, the Caretaker will protect the alcoholic from the outside world. She tries to keep His Drinking a secret. She protects him from the consequences of His Drinking. She pays his bills, bails him out of jail, and calls the boss to

26

make an excuse when the alcoholic is too hungover to go to work.

The alcoholic, of course, learns to depend on the Caretaker's help, because it allows him to more comfortably continue his addiction. And, the Caretaker sees herself as helping him when, in reality, she is keeping herself and the children in a state of strained endurance.

And, behind it all is her overriding concern to appear normal, to seem as if nothing is wrong in the family, nothing unusual in the tension and strained relationships that come from the bizarre mating of His Drinking with Her Caretaking.

Here's how Helen described her feelings in the Caretaker role:

> "Once I invited his mother and father to dinner. I was going to show them how badly he treated me. I picked Friday, because he always went to the bar and got drunk on that night. I barely mentioned the dinner to him, because I didn't want him to come home. By the time his folks arrived, I had carefully rehearsed what I was going to say about his conspicuous absence. Maybe then they would finally understand what I was going through! I didn't think they could change things, but at least they would know that I was 'right' and he was 'wrong.' "

But Helen's attempt at vindication was spoiled.

> "At ten after five, my husband walked in, cold sober, and looking fine. I was so angry I could have shot him."

Helen now can look back and see how abnormal those feelings were. "At the time, though, I was so sure I was right."

The Child Caretaker

As we have seen, Caretakers accept unrealistic responsibility, keep secrets, discount their children, and contribute to high-level stress in the home.

One of the children, usually the oldest, becomes the part-time confidante and fellow-Caretaker with the mother. The child learns the parenting role at an early age. The relationship

27

flourishes when the alcoholic is gone, or is in temporary disgrace. The mother allows the child to assume an almost-adult role, thereby ensuring that the child will fail at both childhood and precocious adulthood.

The Child Caretaker is allowed to know the extent of the user's behavior, and is also allowed to learn the basics of enabling—making excuses for the alcoholic, protecting him from the consequences of his actions, and so on. The Child Caretaker learns about the financial problems, and all the real or imagined consequences to the family. As the position of the alcoholic weakens in the family, the Child Caretaker, in collusion with the mother, begins to assume more and more adult responsibilities, and may begin to contribute to the family's finances.

Eager for approval, the child moves readily into this position. However, the Child Caretaker's position is a precarious one. When the crisis abates, and the alcoholic makes guilty and remorseful efforts to shape up, the Caretaker Co-Dependent moves back to his side, commiserating, condoning, and accepting his behavior—until the "next time."

The next time, she tells herself, will be the last time. The threat comes easy, because she has made it time and time again. And her resolve falters when the alcoholic promises to change —and even does change for a short period. Before long, the next time is right now, the crisis is immediate, and the threat is forgotten under stress.

It's more than possible that the threat was an idle threat in the first place—just one more predictable move in a continuing melodrama of self-destruction and family fragmentation.

Meanwhile, the Child Caretaker is demoted from quasi-adulthood to childhood once more, and is left feeling puzzled, angry and frustrated. He wonders, "What happened? What did I do wrong?" He offered everything he had, and it was rejected.

He begins to feel angry with his mother. She seems to have almost unlimited control—why doesn't she stick by the Child

Caretaker? Can the mother be trusted? Will she always be fickle in her loyalties? The Child Caretaker feels keenly the insecurity now—not only from the alcoholic, but also from the co-dependent mother. He is not necessarily angry with the alcoholic. In fact, he may even have more communication with the alcoholic on a feeling level than with his mother.

This game is played over and over as the Child Caretaker adapts to the crisis pattern. Each time the primary Caretaker abandons the child, he moves to external sources for a sense of well-being. He begins to fantasize about leaving home as soon as possible. When he does leave, he has all the necessary credentials to be an Adult Caretaker.

Recovery and the Adult Caretaker

Recovery for the Caretaker lies in her own recognition of what she is doing to herself and her children. Since her self-worth comes from external sources, she must first see that she needs internal sources of reward. At the same time, she must learn to detach from the behavior of the alcoholic.

What is this detachment? It means taking a more objective view of the family and of the alcoholic within the family system. It means that she must focus her efforts on the well-being of her children, and on devising a new system of rewards for herself.

The Co-Dependent in recovery does not have to give up love and concern for the alcoholic. Detachment is not abandonment or rejection. The Caretaker only abandons her addiction to a behavior that did not produce nurturing results for her.

The very process of understanding that alcoholism takes place within a family system—not just within the alcoholic—allows the co-dependent to begin to establish a foundation for internal self-worth. Further growth takes place as she makes changes, even though she finds the need to change difficult to accept, threatening and unpleasant.

A woman of great courage, the recovering co-dependent

finds the strength to continue and is rewarded as she does so.

As the Caretaker changes the rules in the home, the entire family reacts to the loss of boundaries, the redefinition of family rules. The alcoholic will try to keep the dysfunctional behavior going, for this allows him to keep using the drug.

The children have developed survival patterns and will actively oppose any further change. After all, they have been raised with inconsistency and are experts at countering it, so they will attempt to move back to "normalcy" as they know it.

The Caretaker will use all of her strength and self-discipline to make it through this troubled time. She may slip into the old, familiar patterns, realize it, and then start all over again. She learns that it is all right to make mistakes. She finds that there is much trial and error in learning, and that trial and error is not the same as utter defeat and failure. And, she learns that success does not take place in one fell swoop, but inperceptibly, over time.

Gradually, the children begin to trust this new consistency in her behavior. They will start talking about their feelings, especially in settings where they feel safe and protected. They will learn to become more effective problem solvers, and their own behavior will take on a salutary consistency. The children will develop self-worth more rapidly than the Caretaker, because they have had fewer years of dysfunctional family living.

When the Caretaker first begins to change, she has no intention of giving up the alcoholic partner. She wants to "fix" him. As her self-worth grows, she accepts the fact she cannot do so. She will eventually decide that if he is not willing to accept treatment, she cannot live with him.

This is an extremely important decision, and it involves areas of religious values and financial security, as well as emotional bonds. Faced with the prospect of separation or divorce, the co-dependent must cope with an almost inevitable sense of failure.

It is her decision and she must decide on her own, just as she must accept the consequences and problems that result. She needs a support system that will help her look at alternatives, help her weigh her options, but will also refrain from offering advice. When the co-dependent wife finally decides, she will decide with strength, she will have faith in her own feelings and she will have a sense of growing confidence in her own abilities.

One basic reminder: **Alcoholism cannot exist in the functional home.** Thus, the alcoholic will seek treatment, or he will leave.

Detachment means that the Caretaker must be willing to accept his decision, understanding that she has learned to stop being a controller. She has established communication with her children, and has knowledge of her own worth. She has successfully stopped the progression of dysfunctional family behavior to the next generation.

Linda, a Caretaker, went through a typical recovery process. While growing up, she was the oldest child in an alcoholic home. She was eight years old when her father abandoned the family. She became a Child Caretaker. For years, she controlled her brother and sister, making decisions for them both on financial matters, and on issues of conduct.

Linda became super-responsible for their welfare and their behavior. Her mother was unable to cope with family problems effectively, so Linda ran the household. She became very rigid and controlling. She was the surrogate parent and made the decisions for her mother.

When Linda married an alcoholic, her attitudes continued in her new family. Her anger toward her father colored her reaction to all men, and her alcoholic husband soon abandoned her and the children. It was a perfect, self-fulfilling prophecy. Linda was right about men, and she became rigid in her belief that she was "right." Anyone who differed from her was obviously "wrong."

Linda's resentments and anger became dominant over her sense of responsibility. As she grew older, her children left home, torn between loyalty to her and their need to escape from the tension. All of the kids had to deal with the problems of a childhood spent in a stress-filled home. Two of her four children became alcoholics themselves.

Linda seemed to be two people: One was filled with rigidity and demanded strict obedience; the other desperately sought approval and love.

Linda had great difficulty in admitting she needed to change. She really believed that her behavior was caused by conditions "out there."

With the help of a counselor, Linda grew willing to look at herself from an objective viewpoint, the first step in her recovery. She needed non-judgmental support during this early time. Her controlling behavior soon became unacceptable to her; she began to experience the rewards of change, the rewards of growth in self-confidence.

Linda used her self-discipline and over-achieving characteristics in her recovery. Like most Caretakers, Linda recovered as she did everything else—with great efficiency and total concentration. Her control of her family helped her in establishing communications with them. They were delighted with her change in attitude. They have always admired her, and now they can forgive and love her as well.

Since the Caretaker finds great satisfaction in helping others, the recovery role suits her abilities. If the alcoholic is still in the home, she may set up an intervention with the whole family present. The Caretaker in recovery becomes the woman she was meant to be: helpful, strong, and dependable. She learns to give affection and to communicate feelings.

And, although the family may become fragmented if the alcoholic decides to leave, the Co-Dependent Caretaker in recovery establishes a nurturing system in the family that remains—a system based on mutual love and respect—a system where even amid the slings and arrows of outrageous fortune, there's an ecological niche of joy.

5

The Rebel Co-Dependent

The Rebel Co-Dependent is one who effectively used anger as a survival behavior while she was growing up in an alcoholic home. Long before she matured, long before she dated and finally married her alcoholic husband, she tried to control those around her with displays of impatience and frustration.

Like all children from alcoholic homes, the Rebel Co-Dependent desperately needed the approval and attention of her parents. They were so caught up in their own dysfunctional behavior that they were unable to see her needs. She couldn't compete successfully with the Caretaker (although she tried at times), so the Rebel Co-Dependent looked for another role.

Though bewildered by the many hidden agendas going on in the stress-filled home, the Rebel Co-Dependent was able to see that there was a winner and a loser in each crisis. She learned that she could win more often if she cowed and intimidated the other children. She learned to use her anger and black moods to bully and manipulate. She realized that anger kept her brothers and sisters in a controllable place.

And, she also learned to rely on shame and blame in dealing with others, becoming overly-critical and condemning, rather than positive and empathic.

The Rebel Co-Dependent needed to be an achiever, and tried to take the Caretaker's place. But since the Caretaker was older, bigger, and already firmly entrenched in the role, the Rebel encountered disappointment again and again.

And she reacted with frustration and impatience—which got her the attention for which she longed. At the same time, however, she constantly violated the value system she had modeled after the Caretaker.

The Rebel learned that anger, rudeness and physical intimidation could usually get her what she wanted. In turn, she suffered feelings of guilt. She became confused and angry. As people around her began to fear her behavior, she found herself gaining more and more control.

The world itself took on an angry aspect. She felt hostility wherever she went, and she didn't realize that all those who came near her reacted to her own negativity with anger or fear.

Twelve-year-old Tracy was talking to her aunt. "Tracy," her aunt said, "do you know that you've been angry all your life?"

Tracy looked at her in amazement and replied, "Isn't everyone?"

ANGRY PEOPLE LIVE IN ANGRY WORLDS

Discourtesy was a natural partner to the Rebel's anger. She prided herself on being straight forward and assertive. But, she was really rude and aggressive. To the Rebel Co-Dependent, bluntness and cynicism were far more important than kindness or compassion.

Paradoxically, the Rebel placed tremendous value on honesty and justice. She could not understand that her courageous, often foolhardy, behavior was not always possible for everyone. So she was quick to judge others.

✳✳✳✳✳✳✳✳✳✳✳✳✳✳✳✳✳✳✳✳✳✳✳✳✳✳✳✳✳✳✳✳

Three Characteristics of the Rebel Child

● She believes that she was somehow responsible for her parents' stress, and thus could not gain their approval.

● She feels that she can never be as good as the Caretaker.

● If she cannot get attention in a positive way, then she can always get the attention she craves with inappropriate behavior.

✳✳✳✳✳✳✳✳✳✳✳✳✳✳✳✳✳✳✳✳✳✳✳✳✳✳✳✳✳✳✳✳

Even as a small child, the Rebel Co-Dependent could react loudly and vehemently. It was easier to give in to her than to fight her—she had a stubborn endurance second to none. She could outlast everyone.

When a small child, she'd hold her breath and scream. As she grew older, the Rebel Co-Dependent started biting and hitting other children to get her way, and to get attention from adults. She continued the behavior because it worked for her—it paid off—and, because she had no valid reason for quitting.

And no compromises! Compromise was a sign of weakness.

In treatment, Susie realized she was a Rebel Co-Dependent. She recalled her early childhood: "I can't remember a time when I wasn't angry. Mom tells about my holding my breath until I would pass out. I remember kicking and screaming until my throat was so sore I couldn't talk. When I went to school, the teacher would make me stay in while the other kids went home. After about ten minutes, she would let me go. I would run like hell, and catch one of the kids and beat him up. Their

35

older brothers and sisters used to beat me up, too, but I never stopped doing it. All of my brothers and sisters were scared of me. I never knew the meaning of joy. I was always so angry."

As noted above, the Rebel Co-Dependent is really a frustrated Caretaker, and would have preferred that role in the family. But, since that role was filled, she struck out at the older child, often displaying intense animosity towards her. toward her.

The Rebel Co-Dependent may carry this unrealistic attitude all of her adult life. She is convinced that the Caretaker is superior to her. The Rebel feels that she can never measure up, and since she can't measure up, the Rebel develops animosity toward the Caretaker—a troubled animosity that she spends a lifetime justifying.

The Caretaker, needing to fix and help everyone, often tries to ignore or excuse the Rebel's behavior. As they grow older, however, the Caretaker becomes angry and rigid, and very resentful about the Rebel's criticism.

The Rebel's perception of the older child was often distorted and unrealistic. She was always envious of the Caretaker.

Since her anger was not resolved, it became second nature, a habit. She constantly found ways to reinforce it and to justify it. Whenever she woke in the morning and began feeling angry, she looked for a reason. And she readily found one, for in her high-stress home there was always provocation to validate her feelings. She took total advantage of the dysfunctional behavior of others.

The smallest incident brings out the Rebel's need to criticize and to punish. The stress caused by the Rebel's behavior can be more intense and destructive than that caused by the alcoholic's behavior. **She**, not the alcoholic, becomes the identified problem in the home.

In her teen years, the Rebel becomes rigidly critical. She seeks out peers who reinforce her complaints about the lack of justice in her life. Her friends share her need to blame and to justify their own unrewarding behavior.

The Rebel develops a fine sense of justice, attuned only to injustices suffered by equals or underdogs. And, she constantly criticizes and condemns those who are, in her perception, authority figures—parents, teachers, law enforcement and government officials—whose chief purpose in life is to make her change and conform to their stodgy values. The Rebel also discounts the accomplishments of anyone she sees with the Caretaker's qualities—good students, cheerleaders, club members, and church attenders.

The Rebel spends her life defending her beliefs and actions. When she controls others through physical force or verbal abuse, she feels secure. But the sense of security is superficial, masking a need to have approval of others—a need that is often denied in actions and words.

Sue Ann accompanied her 17-year-old son into treatment. Although she was not chemically dependent herself, she was an angry, controlling mother.

"I know what happened to John," she said. "He wouldn't have gotten into trouble if it weren't for his friends." Sue Ann had a whole constellation of angry rationalizations:

● He was driving because they had been drinking too much.
● He was just unlucky.
● The police were waiting for them—it was all set up ahead of time, just to get John.

Sue Ann's protective attitude—her co-dependent denial and enabling—kept John from learning to accept responsibility for his actions. His problems with alcohol and drugs were explained away, and Sue Ann's enabling prevented him from experiencing the consequences of his behavior.

Children develop self-worth by being treated in ways that indicate they are valued and worthy to their parents and others in the family. Kids need to know they are wanted and respected—they need to know they really count. Words alone don't suffice. Kids can see through the superficial "I-love-you-honey" assurances and the shows of affection that come in a quick hug.

The Rebel child does not develop consistent feelings of self-worth, because of her erratic behavior in the home. She discourages all but the shallowest displays of affection. She does not want to be lovable or huggable. And, although she wouldn't admit it, she does not really approve of herself.

Gwen, a Rebel Co-Dependent, prided herself on being tough, and she raised her children the same way. "Don't ever let anyone get the best of you," she told them. "Always hit first, don't wait for them to hit you."

Her children were the terror of the school ground, and they repulsed any teacher who tried to get close to them or to show them affection. At home, all of Gwen's kids fought amongst themselves, with no boundaries of acceptable behavior given them. But, if one of them were attacked by an outsider, the whole family joined together for protection—or to retaliate. All of Gwen's children believed that affection was a sign of weakness.

In early adulthood, the Rebel child tries to shock the family with her exploits, and ends up violating her own values. During these turbulent formative years, she may experiment with sex and drugs, in seeming disregard of her parents' values.

She uses chemicals with her friends to escape the harsh realities of a dysfunctional home. Her friends approve and accept her behavior uncritically—as long as it conforms to their values. The Rebel thus finds a sense of self-worth in the presence of her friends. She does not find it anywhere else, and so the group becomes tremendously important to her.

She defends this group against all outside disapproval. They are "right," and everyone else is "wrong." "You don't understand me at all," she tells her parents. "You don't like my friends, but they understand me. They accept me for what I am."

But the Rebel is lonely and unhappy, a very real suicide risk. Her constant violation of her values during these formative years often gives her feelings of despair and the belief that there is no virtue in anyone. Perceptive and sensitive to others, she has little ability to communicate feelings.

In these years, the Rebel is often diagnosed as being chemically dependent, based on usage and behavior. She has every chance of being addicted, but may also be misdiagnosed because of her survival role.

In diagnosing the dependency of any alcoholic, the usage history and behavioral history are used, as well as physical symptoms of the illness. Teengers may not have developed significant physical symptoms, so much of the diagnosis depends on behavioral signs.

The Rebel child displays the most erratic, anti-social behavior of any child in the family. She comes to the early attention of the school system or the legal system. It is important that her behavior not be mistaken for chemical dependency. Since she is at high risk for being dependent, diagnosis is difficult to make. The diagnostician is placed in a bind, not wanting to stigmatize the child, yet wanting to offer treatment as soon as possible.

When the Rebel is diagnosed as chemically dependent in her teenage years, she may be sent to inpatient treatment. If this happens, the survival behavior must be identified if she is to recover. It is almost impossible for an angry, frustrated teenager to deal with both chemical dependency and her Rebel-child survival role in a 30-day time span.

In addition to follow-up treatment or aftercare, there needs to be compassionate understanding in the home. If the family she lives with does not see how the dysfunctional family system itself encourages the perpetuation of dependency, rebellion and other forms of family dysfunction, then the Rebel has little chance of significantly altering her own attitudes and beliefs in that environment.

The Rebel who does not develop chemical dependency as she matures, will often seek out a partner who has developed it. A relationship with an alcoholic mate allows her to continue being angry and chronically dissatisfied. Her control as the new co-dependent is based on anger and guilt. She sets up rigid family rules and enforces them with verbal or physical abuse.

Verbal abuse is very damaging to the children who grow up in this second (or third) generation dysfunctional home. They live in a constant state of disapproval, even though the angry Rebel may expend great effort in meeting their material needs.

The Rebel Co-Dependent must keep up a good front. The appearance of normalcy and prosperity is crucial. But the appearance too often belies the fact of a disruptive, and often violent, home life. Physical abuse by the Rebel Co-Dependent is very common, and when discovered, should be dealt with through legal channels. Unfortunately, physical abuse is often condoned by the spouse and the rest of the family as rigid discipline.

Once in an alcoholic marriage, the Rebel Co-Dependent changes the focus of her anger from her own parents to her alcoholic spouse. He suddenly becomes the reason she is angry. His absorption in his illness confirms her belief that she can trust no one, that her anger is indeed justified. She berates the alcoholic in front of their children, even as she protects him from employers and family.

The lessons she learned in childhood help her establish a conspiracy of silence in the new home. Fear fills her when she finally realizes that she is caught in the same trap she lived in as a child. She blames the alcoholic for her unhappiness and insecurity. Oblivious to her own role in the family system, she vents her disappointment on her children and husband.

Yet, the Rebel Co-Dependent also has a need to love her family and to do well by them. She wants to be loved, but she sees her efforts to love and be loved thwarted by the insensitivity of her family. The harder she tries, the more controlling she seems. And the family fears and criticizes her actions. The children make plans to leave home as soon as possible.

The Rebel Co-Dependent has always believed that external forces were causing her anger. She sets up a new system which allows her to continue that belief. While she realizes that her life is unrewarding, she has no ability to see her own behavior as contributing to the situation.

Recovery in the Rebel Co-Dependent

Recovery begins when the Rebel Co-Dependent begins to identify the part she played in her childhood. She must be willing to learn new behaviors that do not interfere with communication. She must learn not merely to control her anger, but to see the source of her rage in her childhood feelings of impotency and frustration. Once the Rebel Co-Dependent can accept that she played a part in the problem, she will take the first steps toward recovery.

If she does not become willing and eager to give up the anger, she will not recover. The alcoholic may leave her, but she will stay angry, for he is not the real reason for her feelings. If a separation or divorce takes place, she is apt to seek out justification in another alcoholic partner.

Confronted with her own actions, she will react in her customary way, with threats and verbal abuse. But, behind her outward show of intimidation, is a woman who is confused, lonely, and in desperate need of approval. Once recovery begins, and she sees that she became angry to survive in an abnormal situation when growing up, she will become able to begin forgiving herself and her parents. The Rebel Co-Dependent in recovery can become friends with the Caretaker.

The Rebel's sense of justice will aid her as she begins this journey. She is a frustrated Caretaker, and has often violated her values with impatience and unrewarding behavior. In recovery, she will begin to look at the rights and needs of her family. She will have to see that her anger was always there, and that she looked for reasons to justify it. The anger, frustration and impatience must become unacceptable to her if the Rebel Co-Dependent is to recover—much as alcohol must become unacceptable to the alcoholic in his/her recovery.

She can now change and become more self-aware. Her self-worth starts to grow with each victory over frustration, jealousy and insecurity. As her behavior changes and she gets positive strokes, she will no longer need the anger, and it will die a natural death.

This process takes commitment, time and devotion on her part. Her rewards will be in the changes she sees in her children and in others that she loves. Having experienced a surfeit of anger in her life, and a dearth of joy, she will be amazed when she discovers a way to release the anger, and to let the joy come in.

If the alcoholic will accept treatment, she will help him in any way she can. If the alcoholic refuses to accept treatment, she may make the decision to leave him. She will do so in the fair and energetic way that is her trademark.

She will learn to bask in the approval of her children and family. She will become the well-adjusted woman she always wanted to be.

In talking about her recovery, Julia said, "I never knew what it was to express love before. I always believed that feelings were negative. I guess that's because I never had any positive ones."

Her face softened as one of her children came over and leaned on her knee. "Now, I'm learning to be happy, and I'm able to feel a kind of joy I never felt before—and a real appreciation of my family."

6
Guilt-Dispensing Saints
and Other Passive Co-Dependents

If a woman comes from an alcoholic home in which she saw herself as an insignificant or unwanted child, she will carry this view into her adult relationships. If she marries an alcoholic, which she is predisposed to do, she becomes a Passive Co-Dependent. Low in self-worth, and unable to express feelings, she has no way to make her needs known to her husband.

The Passive Co-Dependent believes she is inferior to her mate, and always sees him as being more intelligent, more deserving. **His** needs, **his** wants and attitudes assume priority in the relationship.

Her belief in his superior intelligence stems from her own sense of inferiority. She needs to use the attitudes and values of others to compensate for the lack of her own firm value system. In childhood, she relied on the beliefs and values of teachers and peers to guide her. As an adult, she relies on her mate for guidance.

The Passive Co-Dependent has no confidence in her own opinions. Her reliance on others gives her permission not to make her own decisions. She cannot take a stand overtly, so she needs the support of authority to ratify her opinions.

As a child, the Passive Co-Dependent felt shy and unimportant. She learned to survive by withdrawing from the family conflict. Passive withdrawal allowed her physical and emotional control of a small space, a haven. Her pets became her friends because they would not reject her. She learned to live in a fantasy world of "once upon a time."

The Passive child seemed almost invisible in school. She did well in written work, but suffered unimaginable agony when called upon to speak in front of others. She feigned illnesses that allowed her to stay home on those occasions. And she also learned that these feigned illnesses gave her the only consistent attention she got in the stress-filled home.

The Passive Child's Survival Strategies

● The "Invisible Child" syndrome: Shyness and withdrawal, based on an overwhelming sense of personal inadequacy.
● The use of imagination and fantasy to create another reality populated by non-rejecting pets and imaginary friends.
● The use of illness and vague complaints to avoid school and other potentially stressful situations.

******

As the Passive Child moved into adulthood, these survival strategies trapped her in unrewarding relationships.

Passive Co-Dependents fall into two general categories:

1.   The Passive Manipulator (or Martyr) uses manipulative, circumventing behavior to maneuver others into taking the responsibility for decisions, but does not see it as a controlling mechanism.

2.   The Passive Acceptor takes a truly passive approach to life, believing that she has no control over events, and that things will get better if she totally abdicates her efforts to control, accepts the situation, and does not try to bring about changes.

The Passive Manipulator

The Manipulator achieves martyrdom in her relationships, and her martyrdom instills guilt in others. She seems to be helpless and clinging, but somehow she manages to get her way, despite her apparent helplessness. She's an expert at making others believe that her wishes were really part of their plan all the time.

And the Passive Manipulator allows others to take full credit. The Manipulator does not want to make decisions, as she has no faith in her ability to do so. She learns to maneuver others into making the decision she wants made. Thus, she avoids responsibility if the decision turns out to be a bad one. And, since it is not **her** decision, she is not expected to carry it out. The Manipulator learned this clinging-vine, or parasite, role as a child, and she holds to it with great tenacity.

She does not want to be in the spotlight and avoids direct confrontation. She cannot disagree openly with the opinions of others, so she says nothing. But, she has learned to assess situations, and to start controlling them through passive manipulation, before anyone else knows what's going on.

Sarah gives this description of her mother's passive manipulation:

"She was little, kind of delicate, but she had a will of iron. She never yelled at us. All she had to do was look. I would just feel so full of guilt I couldn't stand it. I don't remember a time I didn't think I had to take care of her. We all felt that way, and

I was still doing it until she died last year. Mother was so rigid in her beliefs, so sure about what was proper. She was such a lady, such a good woman. She made us all feel like a bunch of sinners. She always had her way, but it took me a long time to figure that out. I saw her as a guilt-dispensing saint."

The co-dependent who controls with martyrdom is adept at passive manipulation. She lives a life of quiet resignation. She often gives up control of small decisions to end up controlling the big ones. She has never accepted any responsibility for others, and she does not accept responsibility for actions in the home. She reacts passively to situations and events—she seldom takes the initiative.

She places a premium on always being proper and morally correct. She values the opinions of others more highly than she does her own. She cannot say "No!"—and her willingness to assume more and more burdens confirms her saintliness.

The children who live with the Passive Manipulator, or Martyr, grow up with a sense of responsibility toward her. And with a mixed sense of guilt. They have the feeling that she should be **doing** something, but she's so "good," such a saint. Her faults are always difficult to define.

In contrast to the alcoholic, the Passive Manipulator seems justified in what she does. She is not disruptive, she does not cause uproar in the household. Though the children may feel uneasy at her "goodness," they do not see her manipulation, because they have learned that the alcoholic is to blame for the problems at home. They strongly defend the Martyr. She is a "good" woman, selfless and forebearing in the eyes of the world.

The Passive Manipulator, however, lives a life full of fear and indecision. She carries her belief of "once upon a time" into her relationships with her children. As a result, far more than the alcoholic father, she fosters unrealistic expecatations of people and relationships in her children.

The Martyr really believes she is put upon and treated badly. She does not see her own devious behavior. Her alcoholic mate seems to be the culprit. She is the victim—he is in the wrong, always. She is so good and giving, and such an expert at withdrawing, that it is difficult for her to accept that she is causing any of the problems in her home.

When he tries to get her to make decisions, he meets with frustration, for she is an expert in avoiding them. As time goes by, his alcoholism forces him further into rigidity and isolation. He begins to feel guilty and remorseful, even when he knows he is right. His anger and frustration toward the Passive Manipulator deepens, and the relationship deteriorates.

If she is willing to accept responsibility for change, the Passive Manipulator can develop a rewarding assertiveness. She can learn to make decisions for herself and her children. She can establish her own values that allow her to put her own needs and those of her children first. And she can learn to accept responsibility for her decisions.

The Passive Acceptor

The second type of Passive Co-Dependent—the Acceptor—absolutely believes that she is unimportant and cannot control any aspect of her destiny. If she does not get into a recovery process as the marriage goes on, she will lose what little ability she has to assert herself.

The lack of consistency in her childhood home gave the Passive Acceptor little chance to learn decision-making, or to understand the process of completing a project. She has no confidence in her own decisions, and defers to her mate. If he is alcoholic, his decisions will be distorted by his addiction, and will seldom be in her best interest.

The consequence? It's a no-win situation for the Passive Acceptor. Her early experiences did not teach direct communication with others, thus she cannot voice her needs, wants, or dreams with the man she has chosen. Indeed, more often than not, the Passive Acceptor does not choose her mate, but instead **is chosen by him**—and she could not refuse him, fearing that she would hurt his feelings or disappoint others in the family. She was passive and indecisive, and the decision was made for her.

In childhood, the Passive Acceptor spent most of her time in a fantasy world. She withdrew to her make-believe world, her storybook land of "once upon a time ..." This dream world sustained her. When problems erupted at home, she told herself, "This is not reality ... it is only temporary—it will get better by and by, things will change." **Things will change.** That's the Passive Acceptor's motto. Things will change, and it will get better, without any effort or changes on the part of the Acceptor. It will just happen.

The Acceptor carries this magical thinking into her adult relationships. Her faith in a romantic relationship is constantly crushed by the reality of her alcoholic husband's absorption in his own illness. And, as she feels guilty about her failure in the marriage, her own sense of self-worth sinks even lower.

The Acceptor has a child-like faith in the future, believing that somehow circumstances will change without any action on her part. When the marriage continues to fail, the Acceptor feels guilty and worthless, believing that there must be something intrinsically wrong with **her**—otherwise the marriage would succeed. The deteriorating marriage gives positive proof that she is unimportant, that she is an undeserving, unworthy person.

Instead of seeing her husband's illness realistically, the Passive Acceptor is more apt to retreat into a world of fantasy. She immerses herself in television or books, or both. She lives vicariously through the lives of fictional characters or celebrities.

Betty, a Passive Acceptor, was raised by an abusive, child-molesting father. Her mother was an alcoholic. Betty had her first child at 16, and she was never sure who the father was. By the time she was 30, she had been involved in many relationships, most of which were abusive and alcoholic. Betty's 15-year-old son was diagnosed as chemically dependent, and was involved in a felony theft.

On the day of her son's trial, Betty did not take him to court. Her excuse? "I lost the papers that told me when the trial date was." The excuse seemed perfectly valid to Betty.

Since Betty had no parental support, she had moved into the welfare system. She wanted her case worker to make all the decisions, and to take full responsibility for her life. Betty's children were completely out of control and were finally removed from her home and placed in foster care.

All the while, Betty continued to believe that things would improve if she did nothing. And when things didn't improve, she saw herself in the victim's role.

Even if the alcoholic is abusive, the Passive Acceptor may stay with him for many years. She puts up with neglect and utter rejection. She puts up with verbal and physical abuse. Battered, even hospitalized, she returns to the home time-after-time, only to suffer more humiliation.

The children in such a home learn very early that she cannot protect them from physical or psychological abuse. She can't even fend for herself. The kids end up feeling protective and will intercede on her behalf in abusive situations.

Marty was a 10-year-old boy who described his father's beating of his Passive mother.

"I couldn't stand it when he hit her. She wouldn't fight back or run. He shoved her into the stove one day. I ran over and started hitting him on his back. He turned around and knocked me across the kitchen. Then he left. Mom just started cleaning up the mess and then began to cook dinner. I couldn't understand why she didn't say anything, so I didn't say anything either. But I decided that when I got big enough, I'd kill him. I hated him, but I was mad at her too, because she would take it. Then I would feel bad because I was mad at her. When he came home that time, he never said he was sorry, or anything. Nobody said anything about it, so I didn't either."

For the Passive Acceptor, life went on as if nothing had happened. And all the co-dependents in the family engaged in

49

the well-known conspiracy of silence.

The Passive Acceptor may have little ability to perceive spouse abuse and child abuse in her own home. The spouse abuse may be gradual, starting out with verbal abuse, then escalating to pushing and shoving, then culminating in slapping and unequivocal battering. The child abuse is easily rationalized as discipline. In time, the Acceptor may feel uneasy or frightened by the intensity of her spouse's actions, but she has difficulty in judging them correctly.

As the child does not see attacks on the mother as **battering** or **abuse**, neither does the battered Passive Acceptor label her husband's physical aggression toward her children as assault or abuse.

Sheila, for example, was married to an abusive alcoholic for eight years. He was finally accused of molesting and battering her 10-year-old daughter from another marriage. Sheila, a Passive Acceptor, refused to see the reality of the situation. She blamed the school authorities and the judicial system. Even when her husband admitted his guilt, she refused to change her opinion that he was blameless. She insisted on continuing the relationship, even though it meant losing her child.

Sheila was terrified at being alone, terrified at the thought of making her own decisions. When her husband was finally sent to prison, Sheila withdrew from people and spent her time in correspondence with him. She developed a fantasy world of how it would be when he returned home. Sheila never accepted any responsibility for her part in the disastrous situation. And the child remained in foster care.

Life with a Passive Co-Dependent

Children growing up with a Passive Co-Dependent tend to see her as virtuous, the very soul of patience—even as she frustrates them by her inaction, by her passive acceptance of the alcoholic's actions. The Passive Co-Dependent engenders ambivalence in her children, and when they become critical of her passivity, they immediately feel guilty.

She does not mean for them to feel guilty, however. She's often surprised when told that they feel that way. After all, the Passive Co-Dependent sees herself as being powerless, totally unable to control events. She spends her life believing that conditions will worsen if she tries to change them. She is amazed when others have different perceptions about her.

The alcoholic living with a Passive Co-Dependent is constantly in the wrong. He may feel guilt and remorse for his treatment of her, but since she cannot communicate with him, he has no way of resolving his feelings. He becomes increasingly frustrated and vents his impatience in behavior that separates them further—violent drunken tantrums, verbal abuse and more battering.

Samantha was raised in an alcoholic home. Her role there was to be as invisible as possible. She spoke only in a low voice and was afraid of everything. She could not judge nurturing behavior, because she did not see it in her home of origin.

When David began asking Samantha out, she bloomed for the first time in her life. Her naturally kind and loving nature responded to affection and sex. She was not troubled by David's inability to express his feelings, nor did she consider his alcoholic ancestry as being important.

Soon after they were married, David seemed to change. "Why are you always so stupid?" he yelled at her, when she accidentally locked the keys in the car. At other times, he was angrily impatient and he railed at her for being clumsy and inept.

Confused and bewildered, Samantha reacted in the only way she knew how: She withdrew, she quietly moved back into her shell, as if everything was normal. Her friends were uncomfortable in this strained, unpleasant atmosphere, and they soon stopped calling.

David, meanwhile, felt insecure unless he was controlling her behavior every moment. He often accused Samantha of ridiculous infidelities—ridiculous to Samantha, but not ridiculous to David. She tried to convince him that his accusations were unfounded. She would implore him to call her friends and relatives to convince him of her innocence. This behavior seemed normal to her.

The Passive Co-Dependent stays in an abnormal situation long after all hope is gone. She feels unable to live by herself. Samantha was no different. She did not see David's obvious need to cut her off from her friends so that he could feel more secure. As he became more physically abusive, Samantha became more passive. She tried to make everything perfect in the home—perhaps that would help, she thought. But it didn't.

When David mistreated the children, Samantha felt uneasy, but was unable to intercede. She was locked into a living nightmare, and could not reach out for help.

When the neighbors finally called the police, and David was arrested, Samantha refused to file charges—partly from fear of his returning home, but also she believed that she was somehow responsible for his actions. "If I had only been a better wife," she thought, "David would be all right."

With treatment, Samantha began to understand what had happened, and she began to grasp the part she played in making the marriage a nightmare for everyone. She had to learn nurturing family behavior and rewarding values. The therapy group became her support system until she was able to leave David.

The children in these abusive homes soon learn to be quiet and to stay out of the way. They never know what might trigger violence from the unpredictable alcoholic—full of maudlin sentimentality one minute, and enraged the next. And they realize that the Passive Co-Dependent cannot rescue them. As the children grow older, they challenge the abusive parent and then leave home as soon as possible. The tragedy is that these kids often become abusive parents themselves.

The Passive Co-Dependent in Recovery

Recovery for the Passive Co-Dependent begins with the belief that she has a right to have her own needs met and her dreams fulfilled. She must come to see that her passive behavior gives the alcoholic an accepting environment to continue his usage. As the Passive Co-Dependent makes progress and gains small rewards, she gains confidence in her own ability to act. She slowly learns how to risk and to trust.

Seriously battered by her husband, Mary was in the hospital. A counselor visited her twice, trying to help Mary grasp the abnormality of her home life. Mary seemed to listen intently, but the third day she insisted on leaving. "I've got to go home," she told the counselor. "I've got to go home and take my punishment." In Mary's mind, her husband had not **battered** her—he had merely **disciplined her**, given her what she had coming.

Her husband's behavior persisted until an older son beat him badly. He then entered treatment and achieved sobriety. But they didn't live happily ever after—not at first. Ironically, Mary's husband recovered more rapidly than Mary did.

Mary had difficulty seeing that she had any part in the problem. She had never developed enough self-worth to make decisions regarding her own welfare. She always deferred to others, especially to her mother, who had been aggressive and arrogant. Mary's recovery was slowed because of her persistent belief that she had no ability to change, that she was powerless to control her life.

Carol's husband was a maintenance drinker—drinking heavily every night, but going to work every day. Carol's evenings were spent alone. As her husband neared retirement, his drinking worsened, and he went to the basement to drink and sleep.

Carol's children, all grown, begged her to intercede. Finally, a friend convinced her to attend Al-Anon. Once she was exposed to the Al-Anon teachings, she quickly realized that her husband's illness would be a terminal one, if not controlled.

After six months of therapy for herself, Carol was willing to try a family intervention. With careful planning, the intervention worked. Her husband went into treatment and recovered.

Carol's six months of therapy were essential. She learned to make small decisions which resulted in small, but cumulative, gains in self-worth. She learned to identify and expect rewards in her relationships. In many ways, Carol changed more in her recovery from co-dependency than her husband did.

The Passive Co-Dependent needs a great deal of support during therapy. She gives the impression that her feelings are fragile and she will easily retreat to a safer place. "Why are you being so cruel to me? Why are you saying those awful things about me?" she asks with hurt in her voice. In reality, she's as about as fragile as stainless steel. **These co-dependents have to be tough to survive.**

She will need to establish trust before she can become more assertive—a trust that her new behavior, her new assertiveness, will be rewarded instead of punished.

The Passive Co-Dependent is kind, generous and often fun-loving. She is imaginative and spontaneous when feeling safe. Affection and sharing come easily to her. Her sense of humor and loving nature can bolster her recovery. As her confidence grows, and she gains a new-found ability to communicate her needs, the Passive Co-Dependent will bloom in recovery, and her family will share the benefits from knowing a gentle, loving woman.

7

The Youthful Co-Dependent

The Youthful Co-Dependent in Childhood

The Youthful Co-Dependent is often the youngest child, or one of the younger children, in the alcoholic home. Since the alcoholism existed before their birth, the younger ones are most damaged by the deteriorating circumstances. The 'Good Times' are gone before the children are born, and the kids come into a home already filled with high stress and inconsistency.

The alcoholic family becomes more rigid and isolated as the years go by. The conspiracy of silence between family members becomes more intense as family systems break down and become less important. Ordinary every-day rituals, such as meal preparation, become haphazard or the opposite—completely mandatory and inflexible. The young child, caught in rigidity or inconsistency, cannot understand the rules.

Father and mother both foster inconsistency in their children. They do not show them how to complete projects. Thus, the children do not learn the valuable lessons of self-discipline. And the younger child may be pampered and protected so much that she does not learn to accept responsibility up to the level of her maturity.

The Youthful Co-Dependent learns to be "cute" and full of fun. Or, conversely, she is obnoxious and gets her way by throwing tantrums. Either way, she learns to cope, to survive. And either way, she gets the sought-for attention.

She has fears that turn into phobias. She cannot understand the harsh realities of life, and she cannot see that she is blameless for the uncertainties she feels. She covers her feelings with laughter, joking and clowning around. She chatters nervously and moves too quickly—behavior that may get her misdiagnosed as hyperactive.

If this occurs, and she is put on medication, she moves further out of touch with reality. And she learns another important lesson: That it is permissible to cure bad feelings with chemicals.

Irresponsibility becomes ingrained, and leads to a lifestyle of procrastination. The Youthful Co-Dependent becomes adept at the art of putting things off. At the same time, she churns with impatience, frustration and fear—hiding these feelings as she moves into her teen years.

In her teenage years, the Youthful Co-Dependent becomes more frequently depressed, and her inability to cope with her feelings leads to a fear of insanity. She is at extremely high risk for suicide.

Four Characteristics of the Youthful Co-Dependent

● She fails to develop self-discipline because of the inconsistency in her home as she grew up.

● She does not learn how to make decisions, or how to complete projects.

● She covers her fears and insecurities with laughter and humor.

● She does not mature emotionally or accept responsibility for herself or for her children.

The Youthful Co-Dependent Grows Older

She grows older, but she doesn't mature. The Youthful Co-Dependent acquires few of the characteristics of maturity as she ages. She never becomes a grown-up. If she doesn't develop alcoholism, she will seek out a parental figure to take care of her. Often this person is suffering from alcoholism, a repetition of the model with which she grew up.

Immature in judgment, the Youthful Co-Dependent believes that her new lover will put her first at all times, and allow her to continue her irresponsible ways. However, it soon becomes obvious that he is involved in his own illness, and she is not very important to him.

The Youthful Co-Dependent is not a "good" co-dependent: She is not selfless and protective and long-suffering. On the contrary, she has never learned to put anyone's needs before her own. She cannot accept responsibility for her own behavior, let alone anyone else's. She starts planning to leave.

The Youthful Co-Dependent does not stay with the alcoholic for long. She may have two or three children, and then return to the security of her family. Or, she may turn to the welfare system. Still a child herself, she cannot even accept responsibility for the care of her children.

Like the Passive Co-Dependent, the Youthful Co-Dependent does not believe she can influence events in her life. She is passive and tends to drift with the current. Yet, she can be stubborn regarding her own pleasures, and she may freely spend money for clothes or cosmetics, when she should be buying food or paying the rent. "I'm going to be good to myself for a change," she says, rationalizing her irresponsibility.

Her attitude reflects her basic materialistic learnings: She sees ownership—of cars, stereos, and clothes—as signs of success.

The Youthful Co-Dependent is a user of people—she knows how to use the Caretaker of the family. She often becomes pregnant as a teenager. And then she expects others to babysit or care for her children, while she fulfills herself in frivolous ways. She does not assume responsibility.

As she uses up one source of help and attention, she moves on to another, using charm and humor to get what she needs. The Youthful Co-Dependent learns to exchange sex, or the promise of sex, for security. Sexual performance becomes her one tangible evidence of maturity. After all, sex is something grown-ups do.

The Youthful Co-Dependent has little self-worth, and she suffers from overwhelming fear and worry—which she must keep hidden at all costs. Her constant concern about mental illness makes her defensive. She develops anxieties and phobias.

Jean was the daughter of a prominent lawyer. Although he was drug-dependent, he insisted on the appearance of normalcy. Family status in the community was rigidly observed. Jean's mother had the task of maintaining discipline and control in the home. An angry, frustrated woman, she was physically abusive to her children.

Jean was the youngest and has vivid memories.

"Daddy would show me off, because I was so cute, when we had company," she recalls. *"Then, after they left, he would yell at mom—about anything, it seems. After one of these scenes, she would come upstairs and beat me, or she'd hit me with a belt. I was so afraid all the time, but I learned to laugh and be silly. Sometimes that worked."*

Although Jean was afraid of the dark, her parents insisted that she sleep in a dark room—to get over her fear.

"I hated that room, just hated it. I still have strong memories about long, dark nights. I used to dream about dying—just to get away. It was my only escape. Everyone told me I was crazy and stupid, and I came to believe them, started feeling really crazy and stupid."

Now Jean's married to Ed, an alcoholic, who acts just like her father. It's the second time she's married an alcoholic. "I left Joe," she says. "I left him because he acted just like Daddy. Now I've got Ed. I don't know. Maybe I am crazy. Or stupid. Or both."

While she is young, the Youthful Co-Dependent has no trouble in finding a protector. But, as she grows older, her youthful mannerisms become incongruous—she is really a frightened little girl, trapped in an aging body.

One of her children may adopt the parental role, parenting her as well as his brothers and sisters. He tells her what the family will have for dinner, and he usually prepares it himself. He gets his younger brothers and sisters off to school. He arbitrates their quarreling, and becomes their security figure in the home.

As the child-parent accepts more and more responsibility for the other children, he frees the Youthful Co-Dependent from responsibility. He takes charge, and she remains inconsistent and passive.

If the kids are taken from the mother and placed in separate homes, the child-parent suffers great agony at the separation. He believes that he has failed in taking care of them, and that they cannot be all right without him.

He also suffers the loss of his mother, for she, too, was his responsibility. Many foster parents have had difficulty understanding and dealing with this child-parent in his new home.

Brad was eight years old when his mother first abandoned him and his six-year-old brother. For two days, she did not return home. He fed his little brother cold cereal and milk. When the milk was gone, they ate bread. He kept his little brother in the bed so that he would be warm.

When Brad's mother returned, she was on tranquilizers. She fell into bed, and Brad couldn't rouse her. So Brad got himself and his little brother ready for school. The school lunch was their main food for the day.

When they returned home, Brad took money from his

mother's purse to buy groceries. He bought soup that he could heat on the stove and cereal that could be eaten cold.

When his mother awoke sick and disoriented, Brad cared for her. And, all the while, he was full of anxiety and fear. But he took great care not to let his brother know.

The neighbors finally alerted social service workers to the conditions in the home. The boys were placed in separate foster homes. Brad was furious with the people who took him from his mother and brother. "I hate you!" he screamed. "I hate you all!"

Brad felt guilty at not having been good enough to take care of his mother and brother. If he had been a good caretaker, they wouldn't have been separated. He saw the separation as being all his fault. Brad never learned how to be a child. His mother had foisted responsibility onto him, and he had reacted with a maturity far beyond his years. Brad grew up with ambivalent feelings of love and anger toward his mother.

As the Youthful Co-Dependent grows older, her parents die and her brothers and sisters move away. They have their own family responsibilities. She is no longer the focus for their concern.

Consequently, the Youthful Co-Dependent is forced to accept relationships that are less and less rewarding. She is often found on welfare rolls, living a bare and squalid life at a subsistence level.

If she had a strong co-dependent parent, she may spend her life seeking one type of protectorship or another— desperately wanting to be her own person, and not having the abilities to do so. She has difficulty with anything that requires self-discipline, and she seems incapable of spending money or time wisely.

Betty Jean's mother was an alcoholic, and her father was a Caretaker Co-Dependent. Her older brothers and sisters protected her from all responsibility, as did her father.

At sixteen, Betty Jane ran away with an older man. He soon abandoned her, and she returned home. This cycle of whirlwind romance followed by abandonment became a pattern in her life. Each time Betty Jean was abandoned, she would call her father or one of her older brothers or sisters to rescue her. And they did.

Eventually, she gave birth to a little girl. Because of Betty Jane's erratic behavior, one of her sisters adopted and raised the child. Always involved in dysfunctional relationships, Betty Jane married twice and was in several abusive situations.

At 46, she now lives at home with her aging father. She continues her role of dependent child. Betty Jane is no longer cute or funny, but her mannerisms persist. Her hair has turned gray, so she dyes it the same dark shade it was when she was young. It is long and parted in the middle, just as it was when whe was 16. Betty Jane often ties her hair in ponytails with small colorful barrettes as little girls do.

Betty Jane speaks excitedly and flutters her hands when she talks. She often lapses into baby-talk. Since she is sensitive, she has learned to hide her hurt feelings with quick, inappropriate laughter. The neighbor children make fun of her and try to make her angry.

Betty Jane stays in the house to avoid unpleasant confrontations with the children. She engrosses herself in television, living vicariously. And, she has a strong fear of insanity. No one sees the real Betty Jane, no one sees the frightened, unfulfilled woman locked in an adolescent's personality.

The Adult Youthful Co-Dependent in Recovery

The Youthful Co-Dependent has a difficult time changing any of her behaviors. She feels safer in the status quo, even under adverse circumstances, than in trying to change to something new and unknown. Sensitive and easily hurt, she requires great patience and understanding. But behind the facade of childishness is a woman desperately needing to be accepted in the adult world.

The Youthful Co-Dependent can learn to develop self-discipline. She can learn to follow through and complete projects. She must start with small accomplishments, such as being on time for appointments or shopping weekly for groceries. She cannot be expected to suddenly develop responsible behavior, for she does not know how to do so.

If the Youthful Co-Dependent is rewarded with appreciation and acceptance for small accomplishments, she can move to bigger ones.

She has a well-developed sense of fun and spontaneity. It can be used to help her through the often-boring lessons of maturity. She needs to laugh and play. She may even teach her teacher some lessons in laughter and fun.

Out of small accomplishments will grow an improved sense of self-worth and discipline. She can become the mature and fun-loving adult she was meant to be.

8
Recovery

The woman who marries an alcoholic exists in a crisis-oriented, self-deluded state. She doesn't see the reality of the deteriorating family life around her. She is so engrossed in fighting day-to-day brush fires that she can't see that she's trapped in a flaming forest.

If the co-dependent came from an alcoholic home, as she usually does, marriage may be extremely important for her. She may see marriage as more valuable than its adverse consequences—more important than the fact that the personal marital relationship is not a satisfying one.

If she is the Caretaker or the Rebel, she will have difficulty giving up anything she sets out to do. Quitting means personal failure to her. If she is the Passive or Youthful Co-Dependent, she will have difficulty taking the initiative to make changes.

Recovery does not begin when the co-dependent sees that the **alcoholic** has a problem.

> **Recovery for the Co-Dependent begins when she sees her own dysfunctionality.**

Until that happens, she will concentrate on His Drinking. When she sees the larger picture—when she grasps her own dysfunctional part in the drama of His Drinking—recovery will begin for the co-dependent.

There are several steps in the recovery process. First, she must examine her childhood and her value system. She is the only one who knows the dreams and desires she had before she entered the relationship. She can begin remembering her values and beliefs.

When she starts comparing those beliefs to her current behavior, she will soon see that violations of her values have resulted in her erratic actions and feelings. Clarifying and understanding the inconsistencies between her real values and feelings and her co-dependent behavior are crucial first steps in breaking the bondage of co-dependency.

VALUES	VIOLATION	CONSEQUENCE
Honesty	covering up/lying about behavior of alcoholic spouse	Ambivalence, anxiety and guilt in marriage; passivity
Loving	screaming, pouting, withdrawal, sulking, retaliating	indecisiveness, loss of self-respect
Sharing	feelings of rejection & being discounted	rising anger, hurt & despair; loss of self-esteem
Marriage	sexual rejection; loss of affection; distrust	separateness; loneliness, worry & insecurity
Family	neglect, abuse; ignoring needs; lack of communication	distance; self-hatred; guilt

When she sees that her childhood experiences did not allow her to establish adequate self-esteem, she must then look at how she compensated by developing addictions—dependencies on security, sensations and control. She will then see how these dependencies help her manage her fears—fear of loss of love, emotional and financial security, loss of control over others. And she will see choices emerging, real options and opportunities for rewarding decisions.

As she chooses freely from alternatives that seemed insurmountable to her before, her anxiety and fears will lessen. This is the process of detachment.

Detachment

Detachment is a key element of recovery for codependents. It includes:

1. Separating one's own values, feelings and aspirations from those of the chemically dependent spouse.

2. Taking total responsibility for one's own actions and beliefs.

3. Allowing the chemically dependent spouse to take the consequences for his own behavior—no more enabling, no more covering up, no more alibis, excuses, pretenses or lies.

4. Giving up attempts to control His Drinking.

5. Accepting that she is not responsible for his illness, but that she has a responsibility to end the atmosphere that condones and perpetuates his chemical dependency.

Detachment, in short, means moving from a co-dependent, enabling relationship, to a relationship based on mutual respect, honesty, and a kind of caring, oriented toward recovery— recovery for both the alcoholic and the co-dependent.

As the co-dependent learns to lovingly let go, resentment and anger toward her alcoholic husband fade. But, she will find herself feeling a sense of grief and guilt over her behavior toward her children. She will suddenly be struck by an awareness of all the ways she hurt them.

She will recall times when they sought her understanding and she did not heed them. She will remember broken promises, angry reactions, and ruined holidays. In recovery, she has a new-found objectivity that painfully allows her to see that many of the disappointing things that happened to her children were of **her** making, and not the fault of the alcoholic.

But another healthy aspect of recovery—self-forgiveness— helps the co-dependent cope with grief. She accepts that she made mistakes, she makes amends where possible, and she forgives herself.

If the co-dependent can admit to her children that she made mistakes, and that she wishes to change, her children will almost always accept her. Children love their parents, even though they may not like what the parents have done.

Even if the children have left home, reconciliation is possible. Communication must be established on a long-distance basis, and the co-dependent must take the initiative, not wait until someone else makes the first move.

She does not need to do everything at once. She did not get into this situation overnight, but she will want to change it immediately. Reconciliation must begin gradually. She must let it develop naturally, understanding that over the years, the children have developed their own mode of survival, their own patterns of distorted communication. They, too, will need time to change.

As the co-dependent changes her attitudes about herself and her children, she will discover an amazing change in her relationship with the alcoholic. She lets go. She gives him permission to be where he is. She does not have to join him there, nor does she try to bring him to where she thinks he ought to be.

As the co-dependent makes these changes in her life, she is actually setting the stage at home for an intervention in her husband's drinking. Since alcoholics create crises by their usage and behavior, it will naturally follow that her alcoholic husband will provide her with a time of decision. When this happens, she will be prepared to tell him that she will no longer condone his usage in the home. She will also be able to offer him suggestions for help. If he refuses to accept help, she will be in a strong enough place to make decisions that are right for her and her children.

Co-dependents in recovery finally move to a place of **automatic intervention**. Since alcoholism cannot exist in the functional home, an alcoholic, faced with the loss of the atmosphere that protects and condones his drinking, will have to listen to what his wife and others have been trying to tell him. Her actions have been far more important than her words. Many alcoholics, at this point, will accept treatment. If the alcoholic refuses to change, then the wife, strengthened in her own recovery, may be the one who makes the decision to end the relationship.

The whole concept of the co-dependent's recovery lies in her accurate knowledge of his illness, in understanding her own emotional involvement with his illness, and in her subsequent changes to more rewarding behavior. When this takes place, a set-up for change has been irrevocably put into action.

This change in her is very threatening to the alcoholic. He **needs** the dysfunctional family atmosphere to continue his usage. When the co-dependent changes, the alcoholic reacts with anger or with promises to change himself. She must be aware that this is only the "getting back into the house" game: "I'll never do it again, honey. I swear on a stack of Bibles." And she must be aware that if she falters or relents—if the threat of her new behavior is removed—nothing will really change.

When there is no longer an accepting, condoning environment for his alcoholic behavior, the alcoholic must make a decision to become abstinent or to find a new environment that allows him to continue His Drinking.

If he refuses to change, and refuses to leave, his wife and children may decide that they are no longer willing to endure an unloving and unpleasant life with him. They may decide that they're better off alone. The wife is no longer trapped by her passivity. Her old attitude of "staying for the sake of the children" is long gone.

She knows that she and the children are better off in a home that has loving communication and honest laughter than in a home where a conspiracy of silence reigns supreme and life is riddled with distrust, anxiety, and abusiveness.

In summary, **the co-dependent in recovery will:**

1. Break through the conspiracy of silence around the husband's chemical dependency.
2. Learn to plan and expect financial rewards for herself and her children.
3. Pay more attention to the needs, welfare and safety of herself and her children.
4. Be more relaxed and less inclined to develop stress-related illnesses.
5. Become less isolated from family and friends, as self-esteem increases, and feelings of inadequacy and shame decrease.
6. Become more consistent and less erratic in her behavior toward her children and other important people in her life.
7. Live in a world that is more calm and orderly, where reasons, foresight and dependability are the norms.
8. Regain a sense of humor, trust, and spontaneity.
9. Modify her expectations by letting go of fantasies and by accepting the real world, while learning to live competently in it.

10. Regain her ability to enjoy natural highs, and with it, to appreciate drug-free peaks of joy and exuberance, while accepting the fact that life does not guarantee the immediate gratification of every desire.

The woman who marries an alcoholic can have a rewarding, fulfilled life, the same as any other woman. She can be loved. She can laugh and dance. She can have a marital relationship that allows her to share affection and companionship. And she can have loving communication with her children.

She can have all of these things
if she will first have
the courage to change.

Bibliography

Greenleaf, Jael, *Co-Alcoholic—Para Alcoholic*, P.O. Box 30036, Los Angeles, CA 90030.

Cermak, Timmen: *A Primer on Adult Children of Alcoholics.* Pompano Beach, FL: Health Communications, Inc.

Wegscheider-Cruse, Sharon: *Family Trap; Another Chance.* Palo Alto, CA, Science & Behavioral Books, 1982.

Keyes, Ken, *Handbook to Higher Consciousness*, Coos Bay, Oregon, 730 Commercial Avenue.

Satir, Virginia, *People-Making; Conjoint Therapy.* Pompano Beach, Florida, Health Communications, Inc.